THE WORLD'S RAILROADS
PASSENGER TRAINS

THE WORLD'S RAILROADS
PASSENGER TRAINS

By Christopher Chant; edited by John Moore

Chelsea House Publishers
Philadelphia

Published in 2000 by
Chelsea House Publishers
1974 Sproul Road, Suite 400
P.O. Box 914
Broomall. PA 19008-0914

ISBN 0-7910-5561-2

Printed in China

Library of Congress Cataloging-in-Publication Data
Christopher Chant.
   Passenger Trains / by Christopher Chant ; edited by John
Moore.
      p. cm. – (The World's Railroads)
   Summary: Examines the history and development of
passenger travel aboard trains in the nineteenth and
twentieth centuries and describes different models of
passenger cars.
   ISBN 0-7910-5561-2
      1. Railroads–Trains–Juvenile literature. 2. Railroads–
Passenger-cars–Juvenile literature.
   [1. Railroads–Trains.] I. Moore, John. II. Title. III Series.
TF148.C457 1999
385'.33–dc21
                                                99-051667

PAGE 2: The legendary Flying Scotsman,
*emerging from the Kings Cross tunnels,
London.*

*TITLE PAGE: The graceful lines,
sparkling paintwork and polished brass
make this preserved Stirling 8-foot single-
class locomotive a splendid sight.*

*RIGHT: York station in England, and the
green and yellow livery of the North
Eastern Railway company, which ran fast
trains from York to Edinburgh.*

PASSENGER TRAINS

The function of the railroad is to deliver passengers or freight between different towns and cities or, in the case of the latter, between various points in the conurbation. It stands to reason, therefore, that the passenger's initial interface with the railroad system is the railway station or railroad depot, at which the passenger can buy a ticket and board the train when it makes its scheduled stop or, if the railroad depot is the terminus of the line, board the service right at its beginning.

In the period before the Industrial Revolution, land traffic was wholly restricted to the space it occupied in the overall landscape through which it was moving, and this factor continued to be true right through to the particular land transport's destination, which was a town or city. Thus the relationships of the stagecoach to the country and to the city were essentially identical, for this type of conveyance was an integral part of the rural and urban landscapes through which it travelled, and therefore had little impact on them in the fashion that would become so typical of an external factor such as the railroad and the trains that ran on it. This situation prevailed just as much at the

stagecoach's terminus as to the rural and urban roads along which it had moved, for while the stagecoach's terminus was located as close to the centre of the city as was practical, generally close to an inn at which alighting or waiting passengers could satisfy their hunger and thirst as well as secure temporary accommodation, it was for all practical purposes little distinguishable from the building around it except for a yard and double gate, a combination that was also typical of larger urban houses with provision for a coach and the horses to pull it.

In general terms, therefore, land transport in the period before the full advent of the Industrial Revolution was fully integrated into the day-to-day situation of the regions through which it passed, and therefore possessed no aspect of intrusiveness. The advent of the railroad changed all that, for the railroad was and still is so basically different from the areas through which it runs and into which it operates that there is little commonality between the railroad and the populated areas it serves: the railroad's tracks are used only by the trains that run on them, in both the country and the city, and the railway station or railroad depot are so radically

different in function and architecture from the areas in which they are located that they stand out as totally individual establishments.

Arriving as it did after the time that most towns and cities were established and underwent their first periods of growth, the station or depot cannot in general be an integral part of the town or city, although exceptions can be found in the case of cities such as Brasilia, which are to an extent 'artificial' creations in that they were schemed as a unit with the railroad built into it as an organic feature. In general, however, the station had to be constructed outside the traditional limits of the city, meaning that for a considerable period the station was in effect an extrusion of the city, and only started to become a true part of its organic structure as growth expanded the city round and past the station. In the circumstances, it was perhaps inevitable that the region which first grew up round the station was intimately connected with the railroad in both social and economic terms, and therefore came to be both industrial and working class. In many countries this resulted in the area round the station becoming condemned as the rough

ABOVE: *Railway companies quickly learned to provide refreshments for the train journey.*

OPPOSITE: *The early railway station or depot was built after the city had developed, and often stood apart from the city it served, both geographically as well as architecturally.*

and ready 'railroad district' whose population and businesses were located 'on the wrong side of the tracks', and were therefore regarded as inferior by those who lived in other regions of the city.

Given the fact that the railroad is a genuine child of the Industrial Revolution, with its urban environs a natural home for the type of industrial activity that developed as a major force at about the same time as the railroad and for the same reasons, the station is naturally an industrial artefact, and in general the first stations were built from the middle of the 19th century, and indeed generally remain as classic examples of the 19th century's industrial architecture. As a consequence, most of the world's great

stations are largely of steel and glass construction on a base of brick. The particular nature of the station, with its long platforms that had to be covered and lighted by a structure requiring only the most limited of vertical supports, led to the creation of some of the world's most classic industrial architecture, characterized by glass roofs carried in superb cast-iron frames, themselves supported by cast-iron pillars.

A particular feature of the railroad station, by comparison with most other types of commercial buildings of the same period, was its unashamed functionality: the railway station was designed to facilitate movement, by both the trains and the

traffic, whereas most of the other buildings were designed for what might be described as a far more stationary function as the people and goods using the building were essentially unmoving (goods in storage or on display, or workers standing or seated at their tasks) or only locally moving (shoppers) between their times of arrival and departure on foot. In the case of the railroad station, on the other hand, the trains themselves moved through the structure, in the case of terminus stations in and out of the structure, and the goods and people using the train services flowed through the building in a genuinely active fashion.

To this extent, therefore, the station was a classic example of what has inevitably

and in fact unashamedly been designated as a 'traffic building', and the task of the railroad in the movement of goods and passengers was reflected naturally, and without any attempt at concealment, in its basic design and construction.

Notwithstanding the above, its industrial character is but one of the station's several particular characteristics, especially in regard to the urban passenger terminals that constitute the railway station at its apogee. For example, the station was not created as a unitary building designed solely to facilitate the movement of trains: this was certainly one requirement, resulting in the cast iron and glass coverings of the platform areas, but another

OPPOSITE
LEFT: *In the early days, passengers often had to walk across a number of lines to get to their trains.*

RIGHT: *Finland in the 1920s.*

THIS PAGE
ABOVE LEFT: *A local station in Finland, 1910.*

ABOVE RIGHT: *The first trans-Canadian train on its journey. Arrival at Port Arthur was on 30 June 1886.*

RIGHT: *Buffalo-bone pickers and Red River carts at the Northern Pacific Railroad yard in Minnewaukan, 1886.*

was the movement of passengers in and out of the building as they arrived to use the train services or departed after using them. This led to the design and construction of the station as a double entity in which the cast iron and glass section concerned primarily with the trains was complemented by what might be termed a reception area, generally of a more 'solid' stone or brick construction, whose primary task was to allow the smooth flow of large numbers of passengers between the outside world and the trains they wished to use, and in the process provide the facilities in which they could buy their tickets, refresh themselves, and buy small items (food, beverages, newspapers and periodicals) for the train journey.

An invariable characteristic of such a station was its alignment with the open-

fronted train 'half' facing out of the city toward the country and the more enclosed passenger 'half' facing into the city toward roads and buildings. As such, the station fell into two categories with its train half essentially industrial and it passenger half primarily urban. This two-aspect feature of the railroad station in its definitive urban form did not appear overnight, but was rather the result of two decades of initially slow but soon very rapidly accelerating railroad development. The train half of the station did not reach it definitive cast iron and glass form until the 1850s, and was clearly inspired strongly by the technical success and phenomenal popularity in London of the Crystal Palace of 1851, which was responsible for a rapid development of these materials as important architectural features. More important still,

however, was the success of the railroads during their first 20 years of existence, when traffic grew at an unprecedented rate and the railroad operators foresaw no reason that this rate of growth would not continue into the foreseeable future. This growth in traffic called for the creation and implementation of novel technical solutions to problems such as the enclosure of large numbers of parallel platforms and the rapid movement of great numbers of passengers. During the railroad's first days in the 1830s, railway operations were limited to single-line connections between cities, and stations of very modest dimensions and ambitions were more than adequate. Most stations therefore comprised just one platform, separate buildings for arrivals and departures, and a roof that was often of wood.

During the 1840s the network of

ABOVE LEFT: *Train concourse, Penne station, Northern Pacific Railroad, 1909, a classic of cast iron and glass construction.*

ABOVE: *Three Cocks Junction, England, 1962.*

OPPOSITE: *Bassenthwaite Lake station, Cumbria, England.*

railroads both expanded in overall dimensions and grew denser in its original areas to cater for the demands of more traffic, and this placed an increasing burden on existing stations. More railroad tracks now headed toward them, and this meant that the number of platforms had to be increased and their length extended to cater for trains that had a larger number of carriages now that more potent locomotives were available to pull them. The longer and more numerous platforms had to be interconnected so that passengers could transfer from one train to another, and as the railroads were now emerging from their pioneering period, in which passengers had

ABOVE LEFT: *Engraving of the Metropolitan Railway's Aldgate terminus in the City of London, 1876.*

ABOVE: *South-Eastern Railway's City of London terminus at Cannon Street, 1866. The cast iron and glass construction of early railway stations was inspired by the Crystal Palace, built in 1851.*

LEFT: *A view of the city of Leeds from Holbeck Junction, Yorkshire, England.*

OPPOSITE: *The first British monarch to travel by train was Queen Victoria who, in a train such as this, made her first rail journey from Slough to London in 1842.*

been prepared to 'rough it', the larger area of platforms had to be roofed more efficiently, primarily with a transparent or translucent material, to the demands of now more blasé passengers for a higher level of creature comforts such as protection against rain and wind. The answer was a larger station of a new type with a large glass-roofed 'train hall' linked to the 'passenger hall' by an intermediate structure providing access not only to and from the platforms but also between the different platforms.

From the middle of the 19th century, therefore, this definitive type of station becomes a primary feature of urban development, first in Europe and then, at a slightly later date, the eastern part of the U.S.A. Located on the edge of the original, now increasingly the inner, part of the city, such stations were the access to the conduits through which passengers travelled to and from the outlying suburbs and country, and between one city and another. Increasingly from the middle of the 19th century, the city grew very rapidly as the commercial, financial and administrative centre of the region in which it lay, and this spurred the growth of traffic as suburban regions came into existence to provide homes for the increasing number of workers of all types that were now needed by the city. In the morning, trains from the suburban regions converged on the single or multiple terminal stations in the city, the passengers then alighting at what could easily have become a bottleneck before dispersing again by foot or local transport to their places of work. At the end of the

day, this process was reversed as the workers made their way home.

To a great extent the terminal station should thus be regarded as a gateway to and from the city, its architecture accurately reflecting its two-faced nature looking both inward to the city and outward to the suburbs and the country. It might indeed be argued, in over-simplified terms, that the outward-bound passenger's arrival from the city via the passenger hall to the train hall prepared him for the opening of his horizons as his train departed the city for the country, while the converse was true for the inward-bound passenger, whose horizons were steadily contracted as he approached and passed through the station, neatly preparing him for the more enclosed nature of the city with its narrow roads and increasingly tall buildings. To this extent, therefore, the station can be regarded as much as a psychological as a physical gateway in much the same way that the train itself provides an interface between the industrial and non-industrial worlds.

Oddly enough, given the essentially industrial nature of the railroad and all connected with it, and also the unashamedly industrial interior of stations, those who commissioned and designed large stations from the middle of the 19th century were at considerable pains to disavow the industrial connection on the outside of these large buildings. As a result, the great stations of the second half of the 19th century are notable for their neo-classical façades, which were created as an ornamental attempt to disguise the industrial nature of

the buildings' interiors at a time when many urban dwellers were coming to feel that industrialization might have its rightful place, but that this was not in their cities where it might impinge on them directly. This might seem a specious factor, but the neo-classical façades of these essentially industrial buildings did in fact serve a real purpose, for they were aesthetic as well as psychological gateways between an everyday aspect of what was starting to become an increasingly polarized division between the industrial and non-industrial worlds, reflected in the modernity of the railroad station and its environs on the one hand and, on the other hand, the older world of the city on whose edge industry had sprouted.

As noted above, the station thus became a psychological as well as physical gateway between different worlds, allowing easy access between them without undue mental strain. Providing a means of transition between the open nature of the country and the more closed aspect of the city, the railroad and its stations fulfilled a complex role in a fashion that became increasingly complex as time progressed and the size of cities and their suburbs expanded, demanding additional railroad facilities not only for passengers but also for the goods they created or bought, including large volumes of foodstuffs. This increasingly complex physical aspect of railroad operations was reflected strongly in the development of the station from about 1860. Up to that date, there was no means of direct access between the reception area and the station's platforms, the intermediate stage being represented by the waiting room in which the passengers had to assemble and wait for the door to the

OPPOSITE: Grand Central terminal, New York, in the 1930s. As the 19th century progressed, stations were often built with neo-classical façades to disguise their industrial function.

ABOVE: The Baltimore & Ohio Railroad's station at Camden, 1869.

RIGHT: New Street Station, Birmingham, England, 1946. Earlier features of metal and glass construction and a concourse to enable passengers to cross railway lines in safety are still very much in use.

intervening area to open shortly before the train's advertised time of departure. This arrangement was created specifically to prevent the passengers from reaching their trains in an uncontrolled mass as, particularly in the continent of Europe that was as yet only partially industrialized, the authorities doubted the ability of the travelling public to cope with industrial machinery in an unregulated environment. The situation began to change from about 1860, and a direct connection between the reception building and the train hall become increasingly common, in the process

allowing the development of the concourse in which retail outlets soon sprang up. The passenger's progression through a three-chamber arrangement (waiting room, concourse and train hall) was soon modified to provide a waiting room through which no traffic flowed, and the combination of the concourse and train hall through which all the moving traffic passed.

It is this last arrangement that has continued, with developments and modifications to facilitate the rapid transit of an ever larger number of passengers in the peak periods, right up to the present,

OPPOSITE: Waterloo, London, an example of a modern, functional railway station.

BELOW: Two diesel multiple units await departure at York station, England in 1978, surrounded by classic Industrial Revolution railway architecture.

and looks set to remain the norm into the foreseeable future.

Once he had passed the 'obstacle' of the station with its various arrangements, the passenger arrives at his means of transport, which in Europe is generally termed the carriage or wagon, but in North America is known as the car. In the very first stages of railroad travel, the wagon for freight was merely an enlarged version of the chaldron, or mine vehicle of the middle ages, while all but the very earliest passenger coaches were mere developments of the current generation of stagecoaches and private coaches with flanged wheels to keep them on the tracks. Despite the all-too-frequent and invariably unsuccessful experimental variants that emerged constantly, the better type of passenger coach developed for use in western Europe was for some time a flange-wheeled frame (flatbed unit) built up with a wooden structure to provide passenger accommodation in compartments with side-doors: this type of stagecoach body combined three, four or even more compartments on a single railway frame, and first appeared with the opening of the Liverpool & Manchester Railway. The type was probably created by Nathaniel Worsdell, the well-known coachbuilder who had made the tender for the *Rocket*. Each compartment, otherwise known as a 'body', held six passengers on well padded but uncomfortably upright seats. For those with fewer financial resources, cheaper fares were charged for accommodation in an open-sided *char-à-banc* carriage. Both

types are revealed in some detail in the celebrated Ackermann 'Long Prints' of the Liverpool & Manchester Railway. On this railway passengers could pay an additional charge to travel in compartments belonging to the mail carriage, which provided only corner seats. The cheapest fares of all were charged to those passengers who were prepared to travel in box-like wagons which were often without seats and known in England as 'stanhopes'.

In overall terms, the compartmented side-door coach served faithfully and well over a moderately long period, and before long the rising expectations of passenger comfort meant that this type of carriage was being used, albeit with shortened compartments and harder seating, for the accommodation of second- and third-class passengers. More than 100 years later, basically the same type of carriage was still being produced in the U.K. for use on suburban commuter services around the country's larger cities, its primary attraction for the railway operators being its relatively higher capacity on a frame of a given size, and the ease of entry and exit it provided: it must be noted, though, that these later compartment carriages were considerably larger than their predecessors of the first half of the 19th century.

Another option, and one that was favoured by wealthier families not wishing to travel in a 'promiscuous' proximity to other travellers, was to remain in their own private coaches loaded onto and then chained down to flat wagons. The attraction of this mode of travel was its exclusivity,

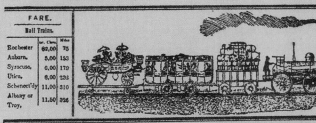

BUFFALO & ALBANY Rail Road.

THREE DAILY LINES.

FARE.		
Rail Trains.		
	1st Class	Miles
Rochester	$2.00	75
Auburn	5.00	153
Syracuse	6.00	179
Utica	6.00	232
Schenect'dy	11.00	310
Albany or Troy	11.50	325

FARE.		
Accommodation Trains.		
	1st Class	2d Class
Rochester	$1.75	$1.00
Auburn	3.68	2.25
Syracuse	4.31	2.68
Utica	5.62	3.46
Schenect'dy	7.50	4.65
Albany or Troy	8.00	5.20

Through to Albany in 25 Hours!

Cars will leave Buffalo for Rochester and Albany, at 6 o'clock, A. M. and 4 o'clock, P. M.

Fare to Rochester,	$2 00
" Albany or Troy,	11 50

THE ACCOMMODATION TRAIN,

Will leave at 12 o'clock, noon.

Fare, 1st Class Cars,	to Rochester,			$1 50
" " "	to Albany or Troy,			8 00
" 2d "	to Rochester			1 00
" " "	to Albany or Troy,			5 00

One Train only will leave on Sundays, at 6 o'clock in the morning.

N. B.—Agents and Baggage Wagons will *always* be in attendance upon the arrival of Steam Boats to convey *Baggage* to the Depot FREE OF CHARGE.

Wm. WALLACE,

Buffalo, June 1, 1843. Superintendent A. & B. R. R. Co.

resurgence of the practice in the form of motor cars loaded onto trains for long-distance or specialized routes, the latter including travel through long tunnels such as those under the English Channel or through the Alps. In this instance, however, the social reasons are different and the occupants of the cars generally ride not in their vehicles but in conventional railway carriages.

What is undeniable about the first generations of rail travellers is that those paying only a third-class fare had a decidedly uncomfortable journey. This was as true of the European as the British rail networks, and a French cartoon highlights the discomfort of the cheaper accommodations by showing porters lifting out passengers frozen stiff by the winter weather.

It was standard throughout Europe during this first period of railway expansion to consider all things American as totally backward or, at best, lacking in an element of finesse. Yet the world owes to the American development of its railroad system a number of important features which improved the lot of the passenger. Thus it was the Americans who introduced, at various times, passenger cars that were both more practical and at times more comfortable, especially for longer journeys. As in Europe, it was the stagecoach which provided the model for the first American railroad cars, but even at this stage differences of practice were readily discernible. As a starting point, the American stagecoach was longer and more

sturdy than the British version while remaining lighter than the French equivalent. This permitted the stagecoach to operate effectively on the U.S.A.'s roads, which were generally inferior to those in the more advanced areas of Europe. It was a comparatively simple task to develop the stagecoach as the accommodation of a railroad car, although a distinctly odd appearance was given to many of these early examples by the practice of adding open seating above the enclosed part of the car. This was typical of the cars designed by Imlay for the Baltimore & Ohio Railroad. Other types of car possessed a body that was almost boat-shaped.

The British carriages and American cars of the early period of railroad development both suffered from their possession of only a short wheelbase, which led to an unpleasant pitching motion in the fore-and-aft plane to the extent that children often described them as sick-making. This led to the rapid redesign of the carriage and car with eight wheels in a pair of two-axle trucks or bogies, rather than the original arrangement of four wheels on just two axles, and this alteration significantly reduced the pitching tendency of the carriages and cars.

Another improvement, coincident with the switch from two to four axles, resulted from the adoption for railroad cars of the pivoted truck or bogie, which allowed a far smoother entry into and exit from a curve. Among the first such carriages was a type built in the early 1830s for the St.-Etienne-Lyons railway in France, but perhaps the

which meant that ladies and gentlemen need not worry about the possibility of dirtying their clothes on seats that had previously been occupied by a possibly unwashed member of the public; but its disadvantages became all too obvious in the summer, when the occupants of any type of open carriage would be assailed by dust, fumes and cinders. As improvements to first-class carriages were made and the 'better' classes of person became more accustomed to the concept of railway travel, the practice of loading coaches onto flatbeds gradually disappeared, and it is believed that the last person to make use of the system was an English lady of the 1880s.

It is worth noting, though, that in more recent times there has been a partial

ABOVE: A Belgian 19th-century carriage which favoured the 'central corridor' of American cars rather than the European compartmentalized side-door arrangement.

OPPOSITE

LEFT: 'Old Number 9', the first Pullman sleeper car of 1859. There had been several previous attempts to create a useful sleeping car, but cabinet-maker George Mortimer Pullman achieved the first real success.

RIGHT: The 'Pioneer' car of 1865, which was completely successful in technical terms and proved immensely popular with passengers.

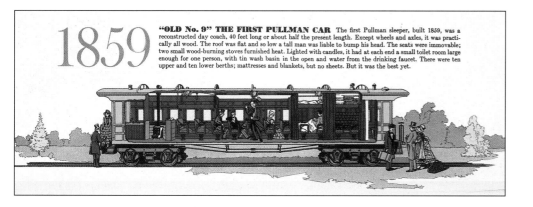

1859

"OLD No. 9" THE FIRST PULLMAN CAR The first Pullman sleeper, built 1859, was a reconstructed day coach, 40 feet long or about half the present length. Except wheels and axles, it was practically all wood. The roof was flat and so low a tall man was liable to bump his head. The seats were immovable; two small wood-burning stoves furnished heat. Lighted with candles, it had at each end a small toilet room large enough for one person, with tin wash basin in the open and water from the drinking faucet. There were ten upper and ten lower berths; mattresses and blankets, but no sheets. But it was the best yet.

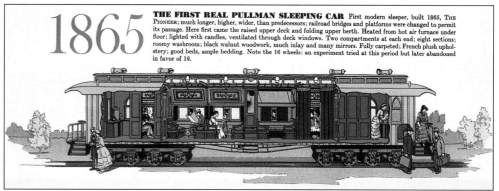

1865

THE FIRST REAL PULLMAN SLEEPING CAR First modern sleeper, built 1865, THE PIONEER; much longer, higher, wider, than predecessors; railroad bridges and platforms were changed to permit its passage. Here first came the raised upper deck and folding upper berth. Heated from hot air furnace under floor; lighted with candles, ventilated through deck windows. Two compartments at each end; eight sections; roomy washroom; black walnut woodwork, much inlay and many mirrors. Fully carpeted; French plush upholstery; good beds, ample bedding. Note the 16 wheels: an experiment tried at this period but later abandoned in favor of 12.

best known is an American car, the 'Victory', manufactured during 1834 by Imlay for the Philadelphia & Columbia Railroad. Between the pair of two-axle trucks was a body of Imlay's typical boat-shaped configuration, and what appeared as a raised clerestory decking was probably a truss-like structure to prevent the main part of the car from sagging in the middle between the two trucks. The section of each truck was enclosed, leading to suggestions, probably fanciful rather than realistic, that one accommodated a bar and the other a lavatory.

Such eight-wheeled cars were clearly the right technical approach to the further development of the car, and during the 1840s they became common on American railroads under the driving influence of far-sighted men such as John Stevens, of the Camden & Amboy Railroad, and Ross Winans of the Baltimore & Ohio Railroad. By the early 1840s these American cars were no longer based so strongly on stagecoach practice, with a number of separate compartments in a fore-and-aft arrangement, but rather on the omnibuses

that were becoming common on the streets of American cities, with a long, single compartment, wide side doors and a central aisle.

By this time the first sleeping cars, though this might be construed as too grand a name, had made their first appearances. Typical of these comparatively primitive early examples of their genre, which appeared in 1836, were the bunk cars of the Cumberland Valley Railroad: the tiered arrangement of bunks allowed passengers at least to lie down at night, though it is probable that few of these passengers actually managed to sleep! A mere two years later, in the United Kingdom, there appeared the bed-carriage on the night train from London to the north-west of England. This bed-carriage was laid out in the standard compartmented arrangement but possessed, at one end, a boot such as the roadbound stagecoaches had for the carriage of the mail. In the case of the bed-carriage, the relevant partition at the end of the adjacent passenger compartment was hinged, and padded boards could be used to fill in the space between the seats so that a

first-class passenger willing to pay the required supplement could lie down with his feet in the space provided by the boot.

The designations first-, second- and third-class were early arrivals on the European railroad scene, and provided an indication of the relative superiority or inferiority of the accommodation provided by purchase of the relevant and differently priced tickets. In the United States, then as now, there was an antipathy to the use of the word 'class' to denote anything that might smack of social difference (and therefore social division), so American railroad advertisements informed would-be passengers that the fare was a certain number of dollars in what were termed the best cars and fewer dollars in what were called the accommodation cars.

It cannot be denied that during this first period of railroad development the passenger was generally faced with a journey that may be described as uncomfortable to greater or less extents, although it is also undeniable that the American passenger soon came to enjoy a higher level of comfort than his European

counterpart. Passenger carriages and cars were not generally notable for the imaginative way in which they were designed or constructed, but it should also be realized that first-class travel in Europe quickly became comfortable if not actually luxurious in the context of what was feasible within the constraints of an increasingly formal Victorian society. This was particularly the case on the services of English operators such as the Great Western Railway, whose broad-gauge track allowed the introduction of wide carriages including comfortable first-class compartments for up to eight passengers on well stuffed leather seats. Even so, there can be no disguising the fact that these early passenger carriages and cars lacked any form of heating during the winter months, had no lavatory facilities for the whole year, or any form of lighting until the later 1830s, when the company introduced dim lanterns that burned vegetable oil.

By the 1860s there had started to appear generally improved passenger carriages and cars, one of the primary driving forces being the desire of the

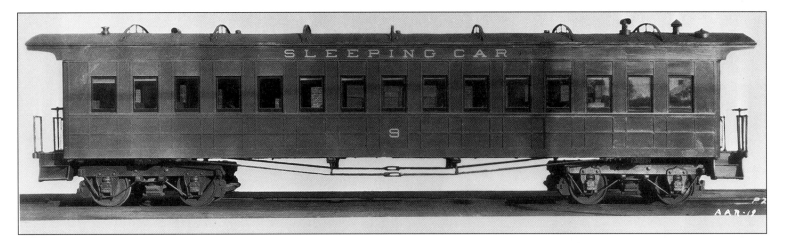

LEFT: *George M. Pullman's first sleeping car, a remodelled day coach. Its first run was on 1 September 1859, from Bloomington, Illinois to Chicago, on the Chicago & Alton Railroad.*

BELOW LEFT: *Interior of a purpose-built Pullman standard carriage.*

BELOW: *Interior of one of the earliest Pullman cars operated on the Union Pacific Railroad.*

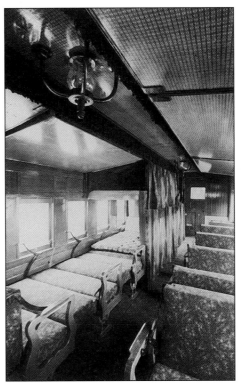

FAR LEFT: The '*Frontier Shack*', the dormitory tap car on the City of Denver, Union Pacific Railroad.

LEFT: '*Old Number 9*', a day coach remodelled by Leonard Seibert and George Pullman into the first Pullman sleeper. The lavish accommodation included ten sleeping-car sections, a washstand, box-stove heater, oil lamps and plush seats.

travelling public for greater comfort with improved facilities on board the train. While the European railway companies opted to retain the stagecoach concept as the basis on which their improved carriages were developed with a steady flow of modifications, and other nations with genuinely long-distance services opted for the omnibus concept as the starting point for their improved carriages, the Americans took the idea a step further and decided to base their cars for long-distance routes on the canal boats that had started the main phase of the American migration west from the eastern seaboard states by means of the Erie Canal and the like.

This was in fact a second step, the first being represented by further improvement of the omnibus type of car with a central aisle that was once disparaged as a long spittoon. The central aisle did at least allow passengers to move up and down the cars, and among the several other positive aspects of this type of car were comparatively comfortable daytime seating in a side-by-side fashion, the provision of a pot-bellied stove for warmth in what could be extremely cold North American winters, a separate but Spartan lavatory compartment, and lighting in the form of candle-burning lanterns that were replaced from the mid-1860s by notably more effective kerosene lamps hung for the raised clerestory roof along the centre of the car's ceiling. This arrangement, replacing the original type of essentially flat roof, kept the lamps well above the passengers' heads, and the clerestory feature also served to provide better light by day and superior ventilation at all times. A feature made possible by the passenger car's evolution from the omnibus was the omission of hinged doors on the side of the car, passenger access and egress being made by means of forward and rear platforms (reached by steps from the ground-level platforms of American stations) with doors opening onto the central aisle. Although the dustiness of contemporary railroad travel meant that serious consideration was the order of the day before a window was opened, even in the middle of summer, the American cars possessed upward-sliding windows, whereas their passenger-carriage counterparts in Europe had downward-sliding windows in their side-opening doors.

Despite its improvements over the first generation of American passenger car, the car of the 1860s was still not very user-friendly. Daytime travel, especially in the moderate conditions of spring and fall, was generally acceptable, but travel by night was decidedly uncomfortable even by the standards of a period more used to adversity without undue complaint. The reason for this was the absence of any real sleeping accommodation, which meant that passengers who were already tired were faced with the prospect of snoozing in their seats. There had been several efforts to create a useful sleeping car, but the first real success was achieved by an American

cabinet maker, George Mortimer Pullman. Pullman's idea was to install folding berths above the daytime seats, which would be modified to pull out flat so that they met in the foot space between the seats, and this would create two levels of berths that could be made up as proper beds. In the course of 1858–59 Pullman modified three day passenger cars of the Chicago & Alton Railroad for a validation of his idea. The Pullman notion proved most successful, but then the American Civil War intervened and it was only after the end of this four-year conflict in 1865 that Pullman returned to the project and produced the 'Pioneer', which must rightly be regarded as the first real sleeping car.

The Pioneer's roof was raised, together with the large clerestory along its centreline, and sliding boards were introduced between the curtained berths on each level so that no passenger would inadvertently kick the head of another. The Pioneer was completely successful in technical terms and proved immensely popular with passengers on long-distance services, and became what was in effect the prototype for all future American development of what instantly became the Pullman sleeping car and provided a level of comfort and privacy that was adequate for mixed-sex accommodation even on transcontinental journeys lasting several days. For those prepared to pay a supplement, there was a pair of private two-berth compartments at one end of the car.

The European approach to the development of the sleeping carriage was

ABOVE: *A Canadian railway sleeping car of 1859. Passengers were grateful for the comfort and privacy of such carriages.*

OPPOSITE: *The central aisle allowed passengers to move freely and lighting was improved from the 1860s when kerosene lamps replaced candle-burning lanterns.*

FAR LEFT: *Advertising poster for the* Blue Bird *Pullman train operating between Anvers, Brussels and Paris, 1927.*

LEFT: *The interior of a second-class Pullman salon (1928-type) operated by the Compagnie Internationale des Wagons-Lits on the* Étoile du Nord *express.*

different, for it retained the compartment arrangement of the standard daytime passenger carriage. Perhaps the best of these European efforts, as befitting the immensely long journeys that might be undertaken in that country, Russia during the 1860s introduced four-berth compartments accessed by a side corridor, and these were ideal for family groups. Some of these sleeper compartments were luxuriously appointed, a factor facilitated by the considerable width of Russian carriages, and a Russian sleeping carriage of the late 1860s could provide five compartments, each with four berths, a central saloon, and above this arrangement an extensively glazed observation compartment accessed by a short stairway. It is worth noting that the Russians were thus the true pioneers of the observation compartment, which next appeared on trains of the Canadian Pacific

Railway in the first decade of the 20th century, and reached its definitive form as the 'Vista Dome' of American railroads in the 1950s.

Another comparatively early European success in the sleeping carriage 'stakes' was Austria-Hungary, a nation of considerable size in its own right and also needing to link its services into an international network providing services from Vienna to destinations such as Berlin. The 'Hernalser' sleeping carriage was essentially a hybrid of European and American features, the former the type of compartmented arrangement favoured by Georges Nagelmackers, the Belgian who became the leading light in European sleeping carriage development, and the latter the Pullman arrangement of seats and berths. Heating was provided by stoves under a floor fitted with gratings, and the central clerestory structure was

American in basic concept but European in features such as its windows and ventilators, which were derived ultimately from stagecoach experience. This type of sleeping car was popular in Austria-Hungary, and also spread to other parts of Europe including Prussia and, to a limited extent, to the Great Western Railway in the U.K.

The definitive form of the European sleeping carriage was created by Nagelmackers, whose success resulted in the establishment of the celebrated Compagnie Internationale des Wagons-Lits (International Sleeping Car Company), which was also known for a time as Mann's Railway Sleeping Carriage Company, Colonel

William D'Alton Mann being a dubious American who injected some capital into the project. The Nagelmackers concept for the sleeping carriage was an arrangement of compartments (with transverse rather than longitudinal berths) opening onto a side corridor providing access to the lavatories.

While sleeping carriages or cars became

increasingly important for long-distance journeys, the type of intermediate-distance journey typical of many central- and eastern-European regions led to the limited introduction of carriages outfitted with *chaises longues* as well as a primitive underfloor heater and a small lavatory compartment.

ABOVE LEFT: The interior of the first-class Pullman salon on the Étoile du Nord express, the epitome of luxury travel of the period.

ABOVE: A 56-seat restaurant car, built in 1928 and operated by the Compagnie Internationale des Wagons-Lits.

LEFT: Three 2-8-0 locomotives with a wedge snow-plough and accommodation coach used in the Grand Rapids & Indiana Railroad, 1905.

27

overall terms, however, the Pullman type of sleeping car failed to displace the Nagelmackers sleeping carriage on European railways.

With comparatively few exceptions, such as sleeping carriages and special ones for VIPs, western Europe preferred to retain the definitive side-doored compartmented passenger carriage rather than switch to the

American style with a platform at each end. Among the British possessions all over the world, Canada favoured the American concept, but Australia and other colonies remained true to the British.

The driving force in the further development of the railways and railroads was the steady increase in the number of passengers. By the 1860s, what is now termed commuter traffic was already considerable, for the increasing urbanization that followed the Industrial Revolution meant that there was more demand for major elements of the workforce to move in and out of towns and cities on a daily basis, manual labourers often being able to travel at a cheaper rate than office staff. The increasing demand for

The French initially adopted a system in which each berth was created by tipping forward a high-backed seat so that the seat was hidden under the now-horizontal back which became the basis of the berth, and the same concept was adopted for the first British sleeping berths, which were produced in 1873 by the Scotland-based North British Railway for use on its services linking Glasgow with London. The idea had only a short career in the U.K., but lasted into the first quarter of the 20th century in France where such a carriage was called a *wagon-lit* (berth carriage).

Typical of many American

entrepreneurs of the period, Pullman soon turned his attention from the U.S.A. to Europe, where his starting point was the U.K. The first British operator of the Pullman type of sleeping carriage was the Midland Railway, which adopted the type in 1874 in a form that was essentially American but scaled down to suit the British operator, and most luxuriously appointed. Several other British railways followed suit, and a good market was also found in Italy for the Pullman carriage which was manufactured in the U.S.A. and shipped across the Atlantic in kit form for final assembly in the U.K. and Italy. In

daily travel was met initially by the use of longer trains with more carriages, but soon the demand exceeded the length of the platforms at which such trains would have to halt, and in some instances passengers were accommodated on two decks to keep the overall length of the train manageable. A pioneer in this process was France, which from the earliest days of its railroad system had allowed a number of operating companies to fit seats on the open tops of many of its carriages. A similar arrangement was also permitted in the United States and was also typical of other countries, such as Austria-Hungary, where the full impact of industrialization came comparatively late at a time when railroads and their stations had already been introduced and platform lengths were severely limited. In the early 1870s, therefore, there appeared in Austria-Hungary a double-deck carriage for third-class passengers who were accommodated in a fairly high level of comfort: the carriage had only modest length, but could carry 90 passengers as 50 on the lower deck and 40 on the clerestoried upper deck, which was accessed by a pair of stairways rising from the forward and rear external platforms. The success of this Austro-Hungarian type of mass transport carriage was attested by its production in moderately large numbers in its country of origin, and also by the fact that its concept was copied, with only limited changes, in Denmark, France, Germany and, at a later date, Spain. France also developed its own double-deck carriage with an open-sided upper deck, but

this type was both uncomfortable (especially in the winter) and dangerous as it was not wholly uncommon for weary or careless upper-deck passengers to fall over the side.

Unfortunately for the British, whose need at the time was greater than that of any other country in the world, such double-deck carriages could not be adopted as a result of the low roofs of the tunnels through which any such train would almost inevitably have to pass to reach a major town or city.

At the other end of the social divide were altogether more beautiful carriages, always better made and more luxuriously appointed than the carriages for the ordinary travelling public. These were the carriages specially made and maintained for the royal families of Europe and the highest-ranking politicians and statesman of the world. The first British monarch to travel by train had been Queen Victoria, who made her first rail journey in 1842 between Slough and London when returning to the capital after a sojourn at Windsor Castle. Soon the Austro-Hungarian, British, German and Russian monarchs, occasionally joined by a French emperor, could call on the services of magnificent carriages, indeed trains, for greater comfort and security on longer journeys. A notable feature of these carriages, many of which survive as museum exhibits after their retirement in favour of more utilitarian but nonetheless beautifully appointed versions of standard carriages, is the superb exterior decoration

to match the sumptuousness of their interiors.

A classic example of the royal carriage that survives as a museum exhibit is that made for the Romanov dynasty in Russia and used mainly on the line between Moscow and Kursk. The carriage had a large and relatively uncluttered interior, but the need for the carriage to convey the Tsar and members of his immediate family in the worst of Russian winter conditions is reflected in its flat rather than clerestoried roof, which reduced internal volume even though it also trimmed the available headroom, the thick upholstering of the furniture and the depth of the pile on the carpet, the careful fit of the windows and doors to minimize draughts, the extensive and effective insulation, and the enclosed rather than open receivers in the lavatory so that there was no problem of icing up or the admission of super-cold external air.

The increase in the weight and speed of trains during the later parts of the 19th century was reflected in the passenger carriages and cars hauled by the more powerful locomotives of the period. The first aspect of these changes was the size of the carriage or car, especially in the U.S.A. By the end of the 19th century the Pullman car of the original American type had become a very much larger item, still manufactured largely of wood but notably roomy, and characterized by its considerable length and weight. Key features of the design, by Pullman employee the great Henry Sessions, included the covered vestibule at each end,

the closely engaging gangways with friction-plate contact for movement between cars, and the large clerestory structure that remained a constant in American passenger-car design for many years to come, as was the arrangement of a central aisle flanked by curtained sleeping berths. Private four-berth compartments, accessed by a side corridor, were available in a variant of the car with a different layout, but the use of such a compartment invariably cost more.

It is likely that the first standard-passenger sleeping carriages with single-berth cabins appeared in the U.K. during 1895 on the east coast express trains operated between London and Edinburgh. Designed by David Bain of the North Eastern Railway, these carriages also offered double-berth compartments for couples. A strong American influence was discernible in the overall nature of the design, which included a large vestibule (with no connection to the neighbouring carriage), and the type proved so popular that it was soon copied throughout Europe, where the Wagons-Lits company later adopted the carriage for its highest-quality international express services.

While in Russia, sleeping carriages and cars were usually of the first-class type only, the western part of the U.S.A. and Canada were providing austere folding berths for impoverished migrants: in Canada these essentially third-class sleeping cars were known as 'colonist' cars.

Another feature that improved considerably in the later part of the 19th

century was the heating of passenger carriages and cars. The U.K. retained a predilection for the metal foot-warmer (heated and then brought to the passenger) on the carriage floor, but elsewhere the stove (sometimes safe and effective and sometimes not) became increasingly standard. Many parts of the U.S.A. can suffer from winter conditions of extreme harshness, and here the standard heater was the Baker heating system, which was a stove-fired hot pipe of the closed-circuit type using water or, in areas of extreme cold, a saturated saline solution that would not freeze when the stove was not lit. Hot-water heating was first introduced in France during 1874, but the most advanced example of this type of heating system was used for a short time by the Great Central Railway in Belgium: developed by M.E. Belleroche as a train-long arrangement using water from the tender heated by an especially developed injector, the system suffered problems with the hose connections, but in overall terms was effective in its primary task of generating heat in the passenger carriages, where copper plates in the floor were heated by the system. A not dissimilar hot-water heating system was used in the Netherlands.

The hot-water concept was quite soon replaced by low-pressure steam heating from a reducing valve on the locomotive, and the first such system to appear in the U.K. was that designed under the auspices of W.S. Laycock in the early 1890s, based on the use of steam piped to storage heaters under the carriage seats.

OPPOSITE: A passenger train of the Northern Pacific Railway at Taylors Falls, Minnesota in the 1880s.

LEFT: Part of Baltimore & Ohio's massive port facilities at Locust Point, Baltimore, Maryland in 1880. Immigrants who had arrived at pier 8 or 9, and been processed in the Immigrant Center (left), prepare to board trains for the West.

BELOW: The first train, a mixed passenger and goods train, crossed over the Missouri river on tracks laid on the ice in 1879.

Another feature that was improved dramatically during this period was lighting. The use of gas for passenger carriage lighting had been pioneered in the U.K. as early as 1863, but the coal gas used in this and similar systems was later replaced by compressed oil gas which superseded coal gas. In the U.S.A. kerosene lamps were still standard, and in Russia candles were still employed. The lighting medium of the future was clearly electricity, and the first use of this to light a passenger carriage was in 1881, when a single Pullman carriage on the route between London and Brighton was first tested. The batteries required for this system were very heavy and required frequent recharging, and it was not until the invention of the J.C. Stone self-generating and self-regulating system at the end of the 19th century that oil and gas lamps were finally replaced by electrical lights.

Throughout the last quarter of the 19th century there was considerable debate as to the relative merits of the two basic types of passenger carriage, namely the European type with separate compartments and the American with a central aisle. The American type was in fact adopted by most countries outside Europe, but even here found favour in the eastern part of the continent and Scandinavia. The prototype for the definitive type of western European compartmented passenger carriage can by found in the so-called D-Wagen introduced to service with the Royal Prussian state railway in the 1890s. This was in effect a hybrid type, for it had vestibules and

gangways like a Pullman carriage, but over most of its length had compartments opening on one side onto the platform, and on the other side onto a side corridor.

The other element that went into the make-up of the typical passenger train in the later part of the 19th century and has remained a standard up to the present is the dining car, which provides waiter service of food cooked on the train. It is probable that the first such car was the convertible diner-sleeper or 'hotel car' of the Great Western Railway of Canada during 1867, but there is a contender in a dining car that was introduced in southern Russia at about the same time. Pullman introduced a dining car on the Chicago & Alton Railroad during 1868, and the first dining car to appear in western Europe was a converted Pullman carriage operated between London and Leeds by the Great Northern Railway during 1879.

A type of organization that was swift to appreciate the value of a railway network to its own operations was the mail service, which saw the train as an ideal transport to replace stagecoaches and riders for the distribution of mail. The first to start such operations, hardly surprisingly as it was the leader among the world's post offices, was that of the British General Post Office. The result was the Travelling Post Office (not only with mail-carrying carriages but also with the facilities to gather and sort the mail while the train was in transit) which was inaugurated during January 1838 in the English Midlands. Within four months of the service's start, further capability had

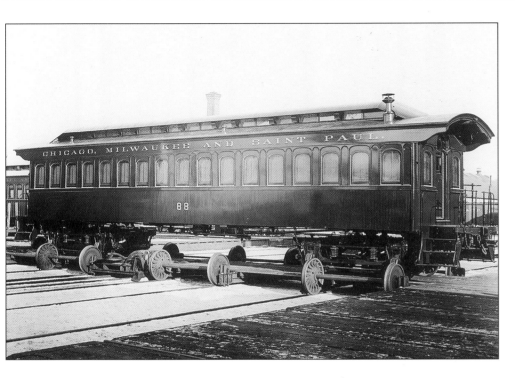

OPPOSITE: *New York Central's* Empire State Express *No. 999 hauls a single passenger car.*

ABOVE: *Chicago, Milwaukee & St. Paul early day coach. American cars had a central aisle and exit doors at each end.*

ABOVE RIGHT: *Atchison, Topeka & Santa Fe Railroad locomotive hauls a single passenger car in 1880.*

RIGHT: *Female travellers enjoying a sing-song aboard a Santa Fe Railroad Pullman in the early 1900s.*

FAR RIGHT: *The compartment-observation car of the Burlington Northern* Oriental Limited, *circa 1910.*

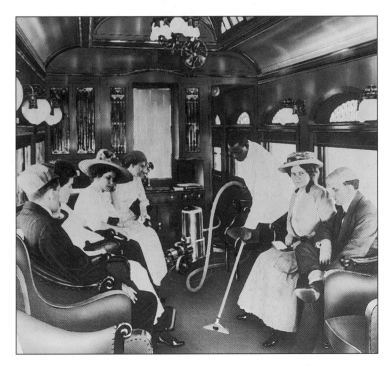

been added to the original transport and sorting of the mail by the development, under the supervision of John Ramsay, of a system allowing the main train to pick up sacks of mail while the train was still moving, and within 10 years John Dicker had improved the situation to the extent that mail trains could both pick up and drop sacks of mail while still steaming at maximum speed.

A similar arrangement was used, albeit on a smaller scale, in Prussia and France. The French travelling post office system was first employed on the route linking Paris and Rouen during 1844. Mail sorting cars were introduced to American postal practice during the American Civil War of the first half of the 1860s, first appearing on the Hannibal & St. Joseph Railroad after the system had been suggested by W. A. Davis. Named the Railway Post Office and rapidly extended as and when the demand justified it, the U.S. postal train held its own on overnight services between cities no more than 600 miles (965km) apart mainly through the advantage it offered, at least until the advent of specialized freight aircraft, of being able to sort as well as transport the mail.

The justification for including a discussion on postal trains when we are concerned primarily with passenger trains rather than freight is the fact that the mail trains are based on passenger carriages and cars adapted for the purpose, rather than on the wagons generally used for freight transport.

The passenger-moving practices of the

late 19th century continued into the first quarter of the 20th century with little significant alteration except in the numbers of passengers carried and the more advanced carriages and cars developed, manufactured and employed for the task. At its lowest level, the movement of passengers was and is one of rail transport's least exciting yet most important aspects, especially when it is concerned with rail-borne commuter traffic. This is the term that has generally been adopted to signify the daily movement of office workers, shop personnel and other workers into the urban area in the morning at the start of the

working day and then out of the urban area in the late afternoon at the day's end. In this context it is worth noting that the commuter is, in the pure sense of the word, a person who, in having to make regular journeys by public transport, has gained the benefit of having his fare commuted to a much reduced sum paid in regular instalments, generally weekly, monthly, quarterly or annually: to the British such a person is a season ticket holder, while in the U.S.A. he is a commuter. But though first adopted in the U.S.A., the concept of the commuter is now universal.

In the U.S.A. the commuter car on the

railroad was at first generally the same as an ordinary day passenger car, and presented difficulties of rapid boarding and alighting at railroad terminals. As a result, in the first part of the 20th century, a number of American passenger-car designers added, in the middle of the car, double sliding doors so that commuters could leave the car at this point as an alternative to the car's ends. So successful was the new type of car that the one used in Boston was adopted in the U.K. by the District Railway when this latter was electrified during 1905. However, the District Railway tried to go one better than the Americans by giving the doors an automatic opening and closing capability, and immediately discovered the dangers of such a system in its ability, indeed propensity, to catch people's clothes, goods and even limbs with decidedly dangerous consequences. After six weeks the system was discontinued.

In overall terms, however, the specialized commuter carriage and car came generally to be accepted as a minimally compartmented or wholly uncompartmented unit generally accessed by a large number of side doors that were either manually- or power-operated.

This division between open and compartmented carriages and cars was not restricted to the trains used only for commuter services, however, but has remained still more important for the carriages and cars used for longer-distance services throughout the world. In the technologically most advanced parts of the

OPPOSITE: The luxurious interior of Union Pacific's Little Nugget, *1940.*

RIGHT: A cook prepares meals for hungry Amtrak superliner passengers. The kitchen, which is air-conditioned and fluorescent-lit, is located on the lower level of the bi-level dining car. Electric convection and microwave ovens afford much more pleasant working conditions for kitchen employees.

BELOW RIGHT: Self-service French-style on SNCF (Société Nationale des Chemins de Fer).

BELOW: The Baltimore & Ohio's Colonial dining car, 1924.

world, the open type of carriage and car has found steady appreciation mainly in North America, Russia, south-west Germany, Scandinavia and much of eastern Europe, while the compartmented type has been generally preferred by most of western Europe and the countries that once formed the British empire and commonwealth. The exception among the countries once under British influence is New Zealand, which has long favoured American railway concepts.

Until a time in the relatively recent past, the most important medium for the construction of railroad cars and railway carriages was wood, at least for the parts above the frame and trucks or bogies. The use of wood was conducive to comfort as a result of its good qualities as an insulator, but presented distinct flammability problems, when lit by gas or kerosene, in the event of any accident. As the travelling public became wholly at home with the concept of rail transport, and began to turn its attentions away from the wonders of speedy travel toward the type of fate that could befall it, there began the development in the last part of the 19th century of a demand for 'safer' carriages and cars. Railroad companies saw in this an opportunity to steal a commercial advantage over competitors who might still be operating wooden carriages and cars. In the U.S.A. in particular, the railroad companies who could afford it and possessed locomotives of adequate power to haul trains of heavier cars, took the opportunity to undertake the rapid design and

manufacture of Pullman-type cars in steel. The railroad operators with smaller coffers had recourse to the expedient of covering their wooden cars with thin sheet steel, the use of large rivets suggesting that the cars were in fact new and made entirely of steel. The fact that the public believed that it was safer in steel cars is indicated by the advertising material put out by the railroad operators: the Chicago, Milwaukee & St. Paul Railroad, for instance, ran an express named *The Columbian* and the railroad's publicity department emphasized the adoption of the new and safer type of car by calling the express 'The All-Steel Columbian'.

Made up of steel cars and pulled by mighty steam locomotives, most of the American transcontinental trains were the epitome of luxury travel: all included bars, dining cars, sleeping cars and a high level of service, and many of them added to this 'standard' level of luxury a barber's shop and, at the rear, an observation car. This latter offered the choice between very comfortable seating inside the car or, alternatively, seating on the open but railed platform at the extreme rear, which provided superb views of the countryside through which the train was travelling.

In overall terms, the standard of passenger accommodation was extremely varied, and depended largely on the ethos and wealth of the country in which the service was being operated. The most comfortable arrangement for an ordinary daytime traveller in North America was the so-called parlor car, which was either a

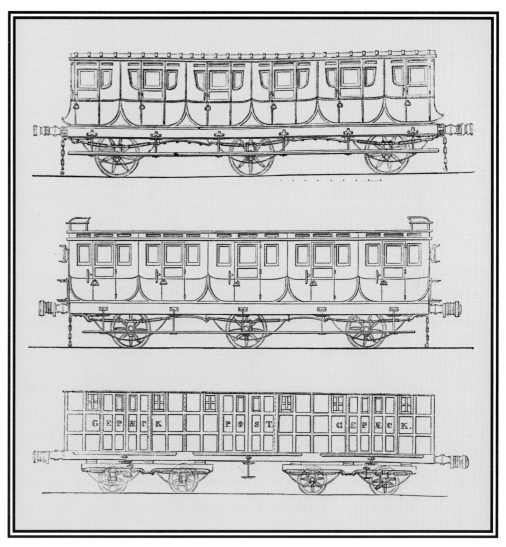

Pullman or a Pullman-type car with well-stuffed chairs on fixed pivots, installed as singleton units on each side of the central aisle. A similar arrangement had been used in the U.K. by several operators, mainly in the south of England, since they had started to import Pullman cars in the mid-1870s. The first British-built Pullman carriage was completed in 1908, and differed from its American counterpart mainly in having single and genuinely massive seats that were movable on legs. Another type of American car was the so-called chair car, which was laid out in a fashion basically similar to that of the day car except for the use of adjustable seats offering greater back support.

The above applies basically to what was known in Europe as the first-class passenger, and the accommodation for second- and third-class passengers was proportionally inferior, in accordance with the reduced fares paid by such passengers. However, in Asia and sub-Saharan Africa the very considerable cheapness of third-class fares was and still is mirrored in the total austerity of the third-class accommodation.

As far as sleeping carriages and cars were concerned, the need for third-class accommodation was met by the adoption of a superimposed trio of berths in each compartment in the carriages introduced in Sweden during 1910: this type of accommodation later spread to Germany, and after that to France. The U.K. adopted

OPPOSITE: The Royal Mail van arriving at the Great Western Railway, Churston, England in 1959. Mail services in a number of countries were quick to appreciate the value of the railway network.

***ABOVE LEFT:** Royal Mail sorting van 80375 at Crewe, England. The Travelling Post Office has facilities to gather and sort mail while the train is on the move.*

***ABOVE:** German and Danish railway carriages circa 1845 show the influence of the stagecoach on early carriage design.*

LEFT: *Richmond interurban car, 1909, otherwise known as the 'Car'.*

BELOW LEFT: *Mack model AR 72-seater gasoline-engined railcar of the Southern Pacific Railroad, 1930s.*

BELOW RIGHT: *Union Pacific's 'The Challenger' coffee-shop diner car No. 393 in the Omaha yards, 1940s.*

OPPOSITE
ABOVE: *This compartment-observation car entered service in 1922 on the Great Northern Railway's transcontinental Oriental Limited.* It had four compartments, glassed-in card-playing and smoking quarters, a buffet and observation-lounge room.

BELOW: *The first General Electric locomotive, built in 1895, shown pulling a passenger train out of the Baltimore & Ohio tunnel in Baltimore. This was the first use of electric power on main-line trackage in America.*

third-class sleeper accommodation only in 1928, in the form of four-berth compartments with two berths on each side. The French had a similar arrangement in their *compartiments à couchettes*, which were in effect second-class accommodations for first-class passengers unwilling to pay the full supplement for the more luxurious full first-class sleeping cars. The Pullman sleeping cars used by the American railroads, which had become mainly of the side corridor type during the first part of the 20th century, had many gradations: the so-called bedroom was similar in standard to the European Wagons-Lits accommodation, while the two still more comfortable and well-appointed

levels were the roomier drawing room and the genuinely luxurious master suite.

A factor too infrequently understood is that the advent of steel carriage and car construction allowed, and indeed almost demanded, a considerable stride toward standardization of basic design, if not the finishing details. It was only in this way that the manufacturers could keep unit costs down to an acceptable level, given the higher cost of their raw materials and investment that they had to make in machinery to press metal panels and complete the construction of the steel car. As the U.S.A. was the main supplier of rolling stock in all its forms to Canada, as well as the countries of Central and South America, the same situation soon came to prevail in these regions.

It was not the same in Europe, where a measure of national and indeed company individuality was more highly prized, and the carriages of the various private and later state railways therefore differed not only in the detail of their finishes and in the paintwork which the Americans generally eschewed, but also in the basic design of the carriages.

Third-class accommodation on railways of the East has generally been of the poorest type, with emphasis placed on the number of passengers that could be carried hanging onto the outside of the carriage as well as standing or sitting in the interior. The third-class carriages of the Indian railway system each comprised a long compartment with four wooden benches, the middle pair installed back-to-back, and

OPPOSITE: Centennial club car decorated in the 1890 motif which was in service on the Santa Fe streamliner Kansas City Chief.

ABOVE: Interior of a Santa Fe Railroad Pullman coach used in the 1930s.

ABOVE RIGHT: Passengers listen to radio and phonograph in the observation car of a transcontinental train.

RIGHT: The footbridge at New Street Station, Birmingham, England taken around 1910. The concept of the rail 'commuter', ferried by train to work in the morning and home again in the evening, was first adopted in the U.S.A., but is now universal.

LEFT: Interurban car No. 1309 at Chilliwack, British Columbia, 6 April 1914. The white flag was to mark the special debut run of this, the last B.C.E.R. car built.

BELOW LEFT: Passenger car built in 1873 by Jackson & Sharpe, predecessor of the American Car and Foundry Company.

BELOW: A lengthy passenger train of the Illinois Central Railroad.

OPPOSITE LEFT: Amtrak's San Diego–Los Angeles San Diegan. Amtrak's standard passenger locomotive from the late 1970s was the F40 PH 'Cowl' Bo-Bo unit.

RIGHT: Sleeper on a Santa Fe streamliner.

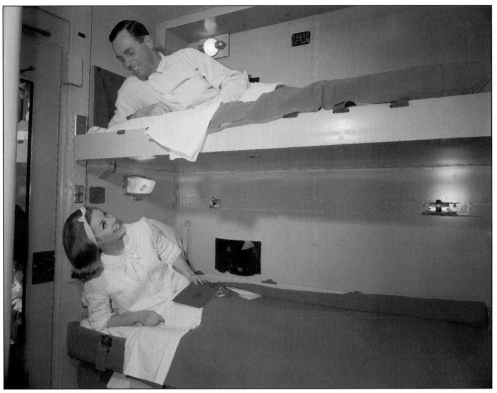

there is only the most primitive of sanitary facilities in the form of a latrine. The same generally applies to the railways of Bangladesh, Burma and Pakistan, although the accommodation in the third-class carriages of the railways in Thailand, the Malay peninsula and Indonesia are somewhat better.

In other parts of the world, the railways of Japan had good rolling stock, based in later years on American design concepts but reduced in scale and opulence. South Africa had several excellent trains, with a class system that was less complicated than that of India (first-class for whites, second-class for higher-class Indians, intermediate-class

for the so-called poor whites, and third-class for lower-class Indians) but until recently subject to the same type of racial limitations that had been typical of India up to the time of its independence in 1947.

The weights of carriages and cars have differed considerably over the history of railroads, depending on the power of the locomotives available and the track gauge of the particular operator, among other factors. Even with the advent of greater standardization, however, there was still a considerable variation in weights. For standard-gauge operation in 1914, for example, the American Pullman in its full glory turned the scales at 80 tons or even

LEFT: Canadian Pacific's famous Canadian *passenger train. 'Dome' cars permitted superb views of the scenic route.*

BELOW: Interior of Amtrak's Broadway Limited, *showing a bedroom in day use in the late 1970s.*

OPPOSITE
LEFT: Amtrak's double-deck coaches on the Southwest Limited *enabled more passengers to be carried in the 1970s.*

RIGHT: Passengers preparing to board Amtrak's Seattle–Los Angeles–Seattle Coast Starlight *in the late 1970s.*

BELOW: A Rohr turboliner carries passengers alongside the Hudson river on Amtrak's Empire *service in the late 1970s.*

more, while the D-Wagen and a typical European dining carriage of the period was about 40 tons, and relics of an older generation might be only 8 tons.

Apart from classics of what soon became established as the 'traditional' national carriage and car types as discussed above with relation mainly to Europe and North America, there were also large numbers of carriages and cars to be found in other parts of the world as combinations of features from two or more of the above with any quantity of local variations. Thus in Central and South America there were North American cars completed with the type of accommodation typical of Indian third-class practices, or British-built carriages with superb seating completed in first-class oxhide, or British-built carriages completed with the American type of seating.

Given that passenger traffic was one of the two primary *raisons d'être* for the existence of the railroad and its locomotives, it is interesting at this stage to look at just a few of the greatest engines from the heyday of the steam locomotive between the start of the 20th century and the outbreak of World War II in 1939.

The French were among the first to appreciate the conceptual advantages of compound expansion for steam engines used in express passenger work, and in no other country was compounding pursued with greater diligence or indeed success. Even so, occasional doubts did enter into

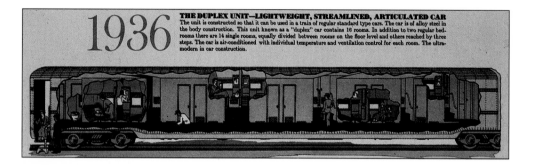

1936

THE DUPLEX UNIT—LIGHTWEIGHT, STREAMLINED, ARTICULATED CAR
The unit is constructed so that it can be used in a train of regular standard type cars. The car is of alloy steel in the body construction. This unit known as a "duplex" car contains 16 rooms. In addition to two regular bedrooms there are 14 single rooms, equally divided between rooms on the floor level and others reached by three steps. The car is air-conditioned with individual temperature and ventilation control for each room. The ultramodern in car construction.

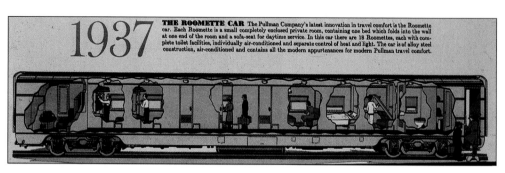

1937

THE ROOMETTE CAR The Pullman Company's latest innovation in travel comfort is the Roomette car. Each Roomette is a small completely enclosed private room, containing one bed which folds into the wall at one end of the room and a sofa-seat for daytime service. In this car there are 18 Roomettes, each with complete toilet facilities, individually air-conditioned and separate control of heat and light. The car is of alloy steel construction, air-conditioned and contains all the modern appurtenances for modern Pullman travel comfort.

the minds of French engineers from time to time, resulting in the manufacture of a group of simple-expansion locomotives, but in overall terms the concept of compound expansion in general thrived and became ever more strong.

This tendency is well illustrated by the 'Pacific'-type locomotives of the Paris, Lyons & Mediterranean railroad. Between 1890 and 1907 the railroad ordered just under 850 locomotives, of which no fewer than 835 were of the compound-expansion type, and in the period between 1905 and 1907 the manufacture of compound-expansion 'Atlantic' type and 4-6-0 locomotives continued unabated. Then in 1907 there appeared the first European Pacific-type locomotive, and in 1909 the railroad produced two prototype locomotives with that type's 4-6-2 wheel layout, one with simple and the other with compound expansion. The availability of these two prototypes allowed the locomotive designers to test and, it was anticipated, reaffirm their belief in the superiority of compound expansion, but at the same time there was another reason for the manufacture of a locomotive of the

simple expansion type. It was known that compound expansion made it possible for a higher proportion of the steam's energy to be converted into work as it expanded, but also that the exploitation of the compound engine's full advantages required a high steam pressure, and that high pressure resulted in increased boiler maintenance requirement and therefore cost. In this second half of the 20th century's first decade, a novel attraction for engineers was the superheater, a system which offered the considerable improvement in the simple-expansion engine's thermal efficiency to the point at which it might once again be a contender for use in high-performance locomotives, which might thus be manufactured and maintained at the reduced overall costs resulting from the use of lower boiler pressures.

The availability of the two otherwise similar Pacific-type locomotives allowed the concept to be evaluated in real operational terms, for the compound-expansion engine used saturated steam whereas the simple-expansion engine had a superheating system. The compound-expansion locomotive had the standard de

OPPOSITE
ABOVE LEFT: *The 1936 Pullman Duplex unit – a lightweight, streamlined, articulated car.*

ABOVE RIGHT: *The Pullman company's Roomette car, 1937.*

RIGHT: *Pullman's luxuriously-appointed coaches soon transferred to Europe. Here a Pirbright is heading west in England.*

BELOW LEFT and BELOW: *In India, railways were developed by private enterprise under a concessionary system, but locomotives were built to a range of standard designs – the BESA (British Engineering Standards Association). These BESA 2-8-0s were more suitable for freight than passenger work, but all coped well with conditions in India.*

Glehn layout of cylinders, with the outside high-pressure cylinders located well back over the rear truck wheels, but the simple engine had an inline arrangement of its four cylinders, as in the railroad's existing Atlantic type and 4-6-0 locomotives. The inline arrangement allowed a much more rigid structure than was possible with the de Glehn arrangement. In other respects the two prototypes were basically similar except for the fact that the compound-expansion engine worked at a higher steam pressure.

The two '231'-class prototype locomotives were used for comparative trials during 1911, and an analysis of the results revealed that the superheated engine developed greater power but also burned 16 per cent less coal than the compound-expansion engine. The next step should

perhaps have been the combination of superheating and compound expansion, but during this period it was impossible to manufacture a superheated compound-expansion locomotive and remain within current weight restrictions. As a result, the Paris, Lyons & Mediterranean railroad ordered 70 simple-expansion locomotives in 1911. In 1912, however, the design problems of the superheated type of compound-expansion engine had been overcome, and 20 such locomotives were manufactured to a pattern that differed from that of the prototype only in its inline arrangement of the four cylinders. For some reason there was still a measure of uncertainty, however, and 20 more simple-expansion locomotives were then made before a 1913 evaluation of the two types of superheated design decided that the

ABOVE: *The* Columbia *passenger train, hauled by a Royal Hudson-class locomotive No. 2860 in British Columbia, Canada.*

RIGHT: *The dining car of the Trans Europ Express.*

ABOVE: *The express* Endeavour, *hauled by a Da-class A1A-A1A diesel-electric locomotive. It ran daily between Wellington and Napier in New Zealand's North Island.*

ABOVE RIGHT: *Articulated carriages are used on some New Zealand Railway provincial services. These cars are built from railcars with modernized interiors. The train is headed by a diesel-electric locomotive.*

RIGHT: *The* Canadian, *the legendary express passenger train of the Canadian Pacific Railway taking heavy snow in its stride.*

LEFT: The Northerner *express passenger train, hauled by a 2,051kW Dx-class Co-Co diesel-electric locomotive, running nightly between Wellington and Auckland in New Zealand's North Island.*

BELOW LEFT: A British Great Western Region Saint-class 4-6-0 locomotive heads a passenger train. Though the first locomotive appeared in 1902, 32 were built before being given the name 'Saint'.

BELOW: Southern Railway PS4-class 4-6-2 locomotive number 1401 hauling the crack Crescent Limited *express passenger train between Washington and New Orleans, in the late 1920s.*

RIGHT: *A number of South American railways bought locomotives and cars from the U.S.A. These two passenger carriages in Ecuador are typical.*

BELOW: *The popularity of preserved steam locomotives has encouraged main-line railways to run a number of 'specials'. Here the Didcot–Derby passes Hatton North Junction in England.*

compound-expansion type offered improved performance as well as a 25 per cent reduction in coal consumption. With the issue of simple- and compound-expansion engines finally settled, the Paris, Lyons & Mediterranean railroad ordered no further Pacific-type locomotives of the simple-expansion type, and existing engines of this type were gradually converted to compound-expansion operation.

During 1921 and 1931 the railway contracted for another 230 and 55 Pacific-type locomotives respectively for an overall total of 462. Within these orders, successive batches introduced gradual improvement, mainly to the proportions of the boiler and the exhaust arrangements, without any major alteration of the core layout. Improvements were gradually made, one of the last being based on the Chapelon package of upgrades to the steam passages and boiler proportions. The Chapelon package was evaluated in an engine which was rebuilt with a boiler having still higher pressure, and although a plan was agreed to retrofit this boiler, only 30 of the locomotives were fully modernized in this fashion, the last of them in 1948, after the Paris, Lyons & Mediterranean railroad had been absorbed into the nationalized Société Nationale des Chemins de Fer. Another 284 locomotives were partially modernized.

These Pacific-type locomotives had prolonged and useful careers, but even in improved form they did not achieve the level of overall performance displayed by the Chapelon rebuilds of the Paris-Orléans railway's Pacific-type locomotives. From

1952, the locomotives were replaced in the main routes by electric locomotives, thereafter spending their declining years on other services. The retirement of the class began during the 1950s, but many of the boilers still had considerable life left in them allowing their use as replacements, and as a result the last of the '231C'-class locomotives were not withdrawn until 1969. The details for the 231C class include two 17.3 x 25.6-in (440 x 650-mm) high-pressure cylinders and two 25.6 x 25.6-in (650 x 650-mm) low-pressure cylinders, driving wheels with a diameter of 6ft 6.7in (2.00m), a steam pressure of 228lb/sq in (16 kg/cm^2), 11,023lb (5000kg)

of coal, 7,397 U.S. gal (6,159 Imp gal; 28000 litres) of water, total weight of 320,767lb (145500kg), and overall length of 65ft 7in (20.00m).

It was only occasionally that any of the world's great trains was hauled solely by a tank engine, but a notable example of this breed was the *Southern Belle*, which was the Pullman express which ran non-stop several times a day between London's Victoria Station and Brighton. Specially associated with this train was a group of seven 'Baltic'-class 4-6-4 locomotives, the most powerful engines ever operated by the London, Brighton & South Coast Railway.

Express services between London and

ABOVE and OPPOSITE: *In poorer countries, such as India and some South American countries, passengers can still look forward to extremely uncomfortable rail journeys.*

the south coast of England had previously been hauled mainly by 4-4-0, 4-4-2 and 4-4-2T locomotives. The new 4-6-4 locomotives were to a design that was to some degree a stretched version of the two 4-6-2T locomotives that had supplemented the other locomotives. Created by Colonel L.B. Billinton, the design was specifically created to provide engines able to haul the *Belle* and other fast trains such as the *City Limited* between London and Brighton in 45 to 50 minutes instead of 60 minutes. In fact, the 60-minute timing was never improved upon, even by the successor to the *Southern Belle,* the electric *Brighton Belle,* which replaced the steam train after 1933; but it had to be recognized that the addition of third-class Pullman carriages to the previous arrangement of just first-class carriages made the train an increasingly heavy load.

The design and engineering conventions of the period were generally followed except in the valve gear, which comprised outside Walschaert valve gear that operated inside piston valves between the frames via rocking levers. The primary reasons for this disposition were Billinton's desire for cylinders similar to those of the 4-6-2T locomotives and the need for a well tank under the boiler between the frames, an arrangement which would have been impossible had there been valve motion in the region. There was trouble with the early units of the class, this including a derailment attributable to the combination of the high centre of gravity and the sloshing of water in half-full tanks. This

accident took place soon after the service debut, in April 1914, of the first locomotive, the *Charles C. Macrae.* The solution to this problem was found in making all but the lower 1ft 3in (0.381m) of the side tanks into dummies, an arrangement which lowered the locomotive's centre of gravity so successfully that speeds of up to 75mph (121km/h) were then quite often attained without problem.

The second unit of the class was delivered just before the outbreak of World War I in August 1914, and five further examples were made in 1921–22. Two more received names at that time, these being the *Stephenson* and the *Remembrance,* the latter being named for the railroad company's war dead and also giving its name to the entire class. The class's later units were never fitted with the feed-water heaters and steam-operated feed pumps which, unusually in British practice, were fitted to the earlier ones for a time after their completion.

After the electrification of the line during 1933, the Southern Railway converted the 4-6-4 tank engines into 4-6-0 locomotives known as the 'N15X' class, a guise in which they had a successful second career on the less exacting longer-distance services of the bigger system, lasting well after 1948 into the days after the nationalization of all the separate British railroad companies into the unified British Railways. The fact that this was deemed worth doing demonstrates clearly the high quality of these locomotives, whose last survivor was retired in July 1957. The details of the 'Remembrance' class include a tractive effort of 24,180lb (10968kg), two 22 x 28-in (559 x 711-mm) cylinders, driving wheels with a diameter of 6ft 9in (2.057m), steam pressure of 170lb/sq in (11.9 kg/cm²), 8,000lb (3629kg) of fuel, 3,243 U.S. gal (2,700 Imp gal; 12274 litres) of water, total weight of 222,000lb (100699kg), and overall length of 50ft 4.75in (15.361m).

If there was a single railroad that set the standards which the rest of the world's railroads generally hoped to emulate, it was the Pennsylvania Railroad. To this extent the Pennsylvania Railroad liked to consider itself the 'Standard Railroad of the World',

and to this extent the magnificent 'K4' class of 4-6-2 steam locomotives, introduced in 1914 and soon the core of the railroad's operations until a time well after World War II, could be called the 'Standard Express Locomotive of the World'.

Following a number of other Pacific-type 4-6-2 locomotives, the K4 class eventually totalled 425 engines manufactured over a space of 14 years. In overall terms, the Pennsylvania Railroad was very conservative in the design and construction of its locomotives, preferring to progress by limited steps before committing itself to a major manufacturing effort, and its adoption of the Pacific-type

OPPOSITE: A Peruvian steam locomotive hauls a passenger train through the mountains.

ABOVE RIGHT: Interior of a French commuter train.

RIGHT: Lack of height restrictions in France has permitted the French National Railways to almost double passenger-carrying capacity on some lines with the introduction of double-decker trains.

ABOVE: Southern Railway PS4-class 4-6-2 locomotive No. 1396 from the glory days of steam trains.

ABOVE LEFT: A South Wales Pullman. From the very first, the name 'Pullman' was synonymous with luxurious passenger travel.

locomotive was prefaced by the evaluation of one 'K28'-class prototype ordered in 1907 from the American Locomotive Co. By 1910 the Pennsylvania Railroad believed that it knew enough about the Pacific-type locomotive to embark on the construction of such locomotives to its own design, and soon 239 'K2'-class locomotives had been delivered. Superheating was applied to these locomotives only in 1912.

In 1913 the Pennsylvania Railroad contracted with Baldwin of Philadelphia for 30 examples of the improved 'K3' class of 4-6-2 locomotives, whose main novelty was the installation of the earliest type of practical mechanical stoker, known as the

BELOW LEFT: Great Western Railway's Cheltenham Flyer, *leaving Swindon station, England, drawn by the locomotive* Tregenna Castle.

OPPOSITE BELOW: Inter-city Paris–Strasbourg train at Lutzelbourg.

'Crawford' after its inventor, D.F. Crawford, the Superintendent of Motive Power (Lines West). The Pennsylvania Railroad had used such a stoking system since 1905 and nearly 300 such systems were in use by 1914, only 64 of them on Pacific-type locomotives. Later stoker designs used a screw feed, but the principle used in the Crawford system was to push the coal forward with a series of steam-powered paddles that were 'feathered' on the return stroke to avoid pushing the coal back again. The coal was fed into the firebox at grate level in a fashion unlike that which later became common, in which the stoker fed the coal onto a rear-mounted platform for further distribution by jets of steam.

Another Alco prototype supplied in 1911 was the 'K29'-class locomotive, which was larger than the K28-class unit. The K4-class prototype of the Pennsylvania Railroad's Pacific-type locomotives was completed during 1914. This prototype, owing much to the 'E6' class of Atlantic-type 4-4-2 locomotives, was considerably larger than the units of the K2 class, offering some 36 per cent more tractive effort and some 26 per cent more grate area at the expense of a 9 per cent increase in axle loading.

It is worth noting that the Pennsylvania Railroad was atypical among North American railroads in aiming for virtual self-sufficiency in the design and manufacture of its locomotives. A considerable asset in this capacity was the railroad's own locomotive testing facility at Altoona, which was the only North American facility at which a locomotive could be run up to full power on rollers. The facility's extensive instrumentation made it possible for the designers' operating and performance estimates to be checked under controlled conditions, and thus for the right modifications to be effected.

The K4-class prototype was tested at Altoona soon after its completion, the evaluation revealing that few changes were needed for the production version. Sustained operational use did indicate the need for a number of modifications and by 1923, with 200 or more K4-class locomotives completed, the hand-operated reversing gear of the earlier locomotives

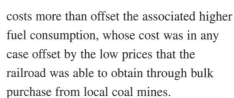

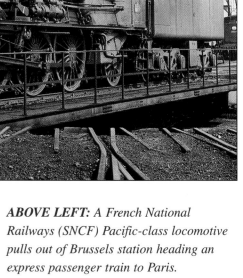

was replaced by a power-operated reversing arrangement. The earlier locomotives were also adapted to the improved standard, and during the 1930s most of the K4-class locomotives were retrofitted with an automatic stoking system to overcome the limitation on power output imposed by the limitations of a single man's strength and endurance. Another interesting improvement of the 1930s was the retrofit of a continuous cab signalling system: a receiver picked up a coded current flowing in track circuits, and converted this into the relevant signal on a display in the cab.

Features typical of the Pennsylvania Railroad's conservative approach to technical developments was evident in a number of features including the low ratio of evaporative heating surface to superheater size, and a boiler pressure only about 75 per cent of that typical in the locomotives of most other contemporary North American railroad operators. This should not be construed as any suggestion that these features were wrong, however, but only that they were different from the norm and geared the particular operating environment of the Pennsylvania Railroad. Limited superheating and a comparatively low boiler pressure, for instance, reduced the amount of maintenance and repair that were necessary, and this suggested that the railroad had decided in overall terms that the benefits of lower maintenance and repair

costs more than offset the associated higher fuel consumption, whose cost was in any case offset by the low prices that the railroad was able to obtain through bulk purchase from local coal mines.

Except for 75 units built by Baldwin, all the K4-class locomotives manufactured during 1924–28 were made by the railroad's Juanita shops at Altoona. There were a few 'special' locomotives among the fleet of K4-class engines. For example, two locomotives with poppet valve gear, thermic syphons in the firebox, and improved draughting were able to develop over 4,000hp rather than the standard 3,000hp in the cylinders, several other locomotives ('K4sa'-subclass units) offered higher

ABOVE LEFT: *A French National Railways (SNCF) Pacific-class locomotive pulls out of Brussels station heading an express passenger train to Paris.*

ABOVE: *A famous French passenger locomotive type, the Class 231K 4-6-2 Pacific, which originally belonged to the Paris-Lyons & Mediterranean railroad.*

cylinder horse power through the combination of the same type of firebox and exhaust improvements with piston valves enlarged from a diameter of 12in (0.305m) to 15in (0.381m), one locomotive was fully streamlined for a while, and a number of other locomotives were partly streamlined. Many types of tender were used, including a few which were so big they dwarfed the engine, but held a larger quantity of coal as well as 23,500 U.S. gal (19,568 Imp gal; 88957 litres) of water.

Outside the railroad's area of electrification, the K4-class locomotives were responsible for hauling all of the Pennsylvania Railroad's express passenger services in the period before the introduction of the Duplex locomotives in the aftermath of World War II. The details of the K4-class locomotive include a tractive effort of 44,460lb (20167kg), two 27 x 28-in (686 x 711-mm) cylinders, driving wheels with a diameter of 6ft 10in (2.032m), steam pressure of 205lb/sq in (14.4 kg/cm²), 36,000lb (16330kg) of fuel, 12,000 U.S. gal (9,992 Imp gal; 45425 litres) of water, total weight of 533,000lb (241769kg), and overall length of 83ft 6in (25.451m).

April 1922 was an important month in British railway history, for it marked the arrival of the first of a new class of Pacific-type locomotives whose record can be matched by few others. Some 79 of what were known initially as the 'A1' class of 4-6-2 locomotives were made between 1921 and 1934 for service on the Great Northern Railway. The core notion at the bottom of the design by Nigel Gresley was that a

substantial locomotive, with more than enough power for the task envisaged for it, would be costly to build but economical in operation over a long career. The thinking behind the design also benefited from Gresley's appreciation that the steam locomotive's primary technical asset was simplicity, and that it was essential for the reciprocating forces to be balanced. This latter could be achieved by a minimum of three cylinders. Despite the basic simplicity of these attractive locomotives, however, they suffered from poor detail design.

One of the poorer features of the design was the valve gear, and this was modified during 1926 in a process that cost little to implement yet effected a major reduction in coal consumption. An appreciation of the need for the changes came in 1925, when a smaller 4-6-0 locomotive from the rival Great Western Railway was tried out on the London & North Eastern Railway, which was an amalgamation of the Great Northern, Great Eastern, North Eastern, Great Central, North British and other smaller railway companies. The *Pendennis Castle*, as the GWR's locomotive was named, managed everything that the A1-class locomotive could achieve, but in the process burned 10 per cent less coal.

The LNER's engineering staff took the opportunity to examine the valve gear of another of the GWR's 'Castle'-class locomotives during the celebrations at Darlington for the centenary of the Stockton & Darlington Railway later in the same year, and then improved the valve gear of the A1 class to the extent that its coal consumption

was reduced by 20 per cent by comparison with its previous figure. The reduction in coal consumption was sufficient for a locomotive of the A1 class to haul an express passenger train from London to Newcastle without the engine change that had previously been required. At much the same time as the valve gear was altered, a boiler type intended for operation at higher pressure was introduced, in some cases combined with a reduction of cylinder diameter. The change added six tons to the locomotive's weight and two tons to its axle loading, but the overall result was worth it and the locomotives fitted with these boilers were designated as the 'A3' class of what was sometimes known as 'Super-Pacific' engines.

From 1928 these locomotives were able to undertake the longest non-stop journey in the world, namely the 393 miles (632km) between London and Edinburgh, with the aid of special corridor tenders so that crews could be changed en route. In 1935 one of the locomotives made a high-speed run from London to Newcastle to test the way for the planned *Silver Jubilee* express with a 240-minute schedule, and covered the distance of 268 miles (432km) in only 3 hours 50 minutes at an average speed of 69.9mph (112.5km/h). On the return journey, the locomotive reached 108mph (174km/h) on the straight and level stretch at Essendine north of Peterborough, and this speed is still thought to be the world record for an unstreamlined steam locomotive. The streamlined version of the A1 class entered service to operate on the new high-speed

service, and the arrival of the streamlined locomotives allowed the older 4-6-2 locomotives to be displaced from their prime position on the East Coast main line.

The demands of rail transport in World War II resulted in the operation of 24-coach trains on the East Coast main line, and the excellent performance of the A3 and surviving A1-class locomotives was an eloquent testimony to the brilliance of their concept but also, as a result of poorer maintenance, of their poor detail design. After the war, efforts were made to remedy the worst of the poor design features, but progress was slowed by resistance from the design office, which felt that the locomotives were essentially right. The classes were widely used to 1965, and the last was retired only in 1965. The details of the A1-class locomotive included a tractive effort of 29,385lb (13329kg), three 20 x 26-in (508 x 660-mm) cylinders, driving wheels with a diameter of 6ft 10in (2.03m), steam pressure of 180lb/sq in (12.6kg/cm²), 17,920lb (8129kg) of fuel, 6,005 U.S. gal (5,000 Imp gal; 22730 litres) of water, total weight of 332,000lb (150595kg), and overall length of 70ft 5in (21.46m).

After the end of World War I many Prussian locomotives, most especially the 4-6-0 units of the 'P8' class, were delivered to members of the victorious Allied powers as part of Germany's war reparations. Germany started a programme to make good these losses to its own railroad system, and in 1919 began work on a 2-8-2 locomotive for secondary passenger traffic in Germany's hillier regions. Work on the

LEFT: *A streamlined 05-class locomotive leaves the Borsig works on its first outing in 1935. These record-breaking locomotives headed Germany's prestige passenger trains.*

ABOVE: *The famous* Flying Hamburger, *a two-car diesel express passenger train which, from 1933, ran between Berlin and Hamburg.*

'P10' class of 2-8-2 locomotives was delayed by a number of post-war difficulties, and although it had been designed more specifically for service on the Prussian railroad network, the German state railway had come into existence by the time the first locomotive was completed by Borsig during 1922.

The design in general drew on Prussian locomotive thinking in the previous 20 years, but the single class that had the highest influence on the design was the 'G12' class of three-cylinder 2-10-0 locomotives, built in 1917 to meet the urgent need for a powerful goods engine for lines of medium axle load. To speed the design process, the G12-class locomotive was based on a Henschel design for the Turkish railroad, and it introduced some novel features to a Prussian design, particularly bar frames and a Belpaire firebox with a trapezoidal grate above the driving wheels.

These G12-class design features were translated into the P10-class locomotive, which also had three cylinders. The use of larger driving wheels meant that there was not enough clearance for the firebox to be installed above the driving wheels, so the grate was made in three sections: the parallel front part was located between the rear driving wheels, the intermediate part was outwardly tapered, and the rear part was parallel and the same in width as the widest portion of the intermediate part. The arrangement set the firebox farther forward, and thus gave a better weight distribution with more weight on the driving wheels, but the resultant complex shape of the firebox walls resulted in maintenance problems and the concept was not repeated.

In the German state railway system the P10-class locomotives were reclassified as '39'-class units, of which some 260 were manufactured between 1922 and 1927. Though classified as secondary passenger engines, the P10-class locomotives were in fact true mixed-traffic engines, and they continued to share their time between passenger and freight work until the disappearance of the last unit during 1967.

After World War II the survivors of the class were split between East and West Germany, 85 of the East German engines being rebuilt with new boilers, round-topped fireboxes and wide grates. In overall terms, the P10 class should be regarded as the apogee of Prussian steam locomotive design, but it was also important as marking the transition to the German state standard locomotives, experience with the P10 class being available before the design of the standard locomotives was finally settled upon.

The American 'Mountain'-class locomotives, more formally designated as the '4300' class of 4-8-2 steam locomotives, were very aptly named as they were used on the steep gradients typical of the operations of the Southern Pacific Railroad based in California. Such a route network demanded considerable tractive effort but only modest overall power output, and this was particularly relevant to the Southern Pacific Railroad, for its eastward-bound trains from Sacramento had to climb over the Sierras, in the process ascending from little above sea level to an altitude of 6,885ft (2100m) in the course of some 80 miles (128km). The Southern Pacific Railroad approached the American Locomotive Co. of Schenectady in 1923 for the manufacture of an initial group of 4-8-2 locomotives to a design that was firmly rooted in standard American design thinking and included a booster engine, driving the rear carrying wheels, to provide an additional 10,000lb (4536kg) of tractive effort.

The 4300-class locomotives burned oil, and the 77 engines of the class (all but a few built by the Southern Pacific Railroad's own plant at Sacramento) were very successful. The details of the 4300-class locomotive included a tractive effort of 57,100lb (25901kg), two 28 x 30-in (711 x 762-mm) cylinders, driving wheels with a diameter of 6ft 1.5in (1,867m), steam pressure of 210lb/sq in (14.8kg/cm^2), 4,700 U.S. gal (3,914 Imp gal; 17791 litres) of fuel, 8,327 Imp gal; 10,000 U.S. gal (37854 litres) of water, total weight of 611,000lb (277150kg), and overall length of 97ft 9in (27.794m).

After the nationalization of the German state railway organizations in 1922, a Central Locomotive Design Section was established under the control of Dr. R.P. Wagner, whose first task was the creation of standard locomotives based on the Prussian concept of the steam locomotive but taking into account the fact that the type would have to operate in all parts of Germany, and would therefore need the ability to operate effectively on low-grade coal and also to climb gradients steeper than those of Prussia. This demanded the incorporation of larger grates and, in the engines with trailing carrying wheels, a clear space under the firebox for the entry of air and the removal of ashes.

The first of the classes were a pair of Pacific types designated as the '01' and '02' classes, which were basically similar in concept except for the fact that the locomotives of the 01 and 02 classes were of the simple- and compound-expansion type (with two and four cylinders) respectively. Some 10 examples of each class were initially manufactured for trials in several parts of Germany, resulting in the decision to standardize the 01 class as this was cheaper to build and maintain even though the fuel consumption of the 02 class was smaller.

The 01 class was basically simple in concept but comparatively complex in detail, especially as there was a range of auxiliary equipment including a feedwater heater with its heat exchanger in the smokebox ahead of the chimney. The detail design of the 01-class locomotive was the work of the Borsig company of Berlin, and manufacture was initially entrusted to Borsig and AEG. The first engines were completed in 1926, and by 1938 some 231 new engines had been produced, a figure to which must be added the 10 02-class units converted to 01-class standard.

Practical experience with the first engines to be placed in service suggested that later engines have cylinders increased in diameter from 25.6in (650mm) to 26in (660mm), the boiler tubes lengthened in a fashion made possible by the shortening of the smokebox, and as a final step the copper firebox replaced by a steel unit. Other changes included better brakes and larger truck wheels, allowing an increase in the maximum speed from 75mph (120km/h) to 81mph (130km/h).

In the meantime, during 1930, a slightly scaled-down version of the 01 class, designated as the '03' class, had been introduced for lines still limited to a 39,683-lb (18000-kg) axle loading rather than the 44,092-lb (20000-kg) axle loading of the tracks that could be used by the locomotives of the 01 class, and 298 of these smaller engines were built up to 1937.

The speed limit on most German railroad lines was 62mph (100km/h) up to 1937, when it was increased to 75mph (120km/h), so it was not until this date that the 01- and 03-class locomotives were able to reveal their real capabilities. The speed limit was further increased in 1939, and when additional locomotives were manufactured a maximum speed of 93mph (150km/h) was demanded. In the light of the German railroad's experience with the '05' class of 4-6-4 locomotives, the new engines were fully streamlined and given a three-cylinder motive system. These new units were designated as '01-10'- and '03-10'-class locomotives, of which 55 and 60 respectively were completed between 1939

and 1941, only the exigencies of World War II reducing these totals from the originally planned figures of 250 and 140 respectively. These were the last new series-built express steam locomotives built in Germany.

Soon after the end of World War II, 70 and 171 01-class locomotives were in service in East Germany and West Germany respectively. Of these 35 East German and 55 West German engines were rebuilt. The last West German locomotives of this family were retired during 1973, but several of the East German units were operated into the first part of the 1980s, returned to

regular service in an effort to overcome East Germany's shortage of oil. These were the last express steam locomotives in Europe. The details for the 01-class locomotive included a tractive effort of 35,656lb (16174kg), two 23.6 x 26-in (600 x 660-mm) cylinders, driving wheels with a diameter of 6ft 6.7in (2.00m), steam pressure of 228lb/sq in (16kg/cm^2), 22,046lb (10000kg) of fuel, 9,008 U.S. gal (7,501 Imp gal; 34100 litres) of water, total weight of 240,300lb (109000kg) without the tender, and overall length of 78ft 6in (23.94m).

ABOVE: Modern German Railway (Deutsche Bundesbahn) main-line trains.

OPPOSITE: A German Class 01 4-6-2 steam locomotive, which headed the most important German steam trains in its day.

Picture Acknowledgements

*Amtrak: pages 43 left, 44 right, 45 all
*Atchison, Topeka & Santa Fe Railway: pages 33 top right and below left, 41 top left
*Baltimore & Ohio Railroad: pages 6, 15 left, 31 top, 35 below left
*Belgian Railways: page 18 top left
*Bundesarchiv: page 60 both
*Burlington Northern Railroad: pages 33 below right, 39 top
*Canadian National: pages 24, 25, 41 top right
*Canadian Pacific Corporate Archives: 44 left, 49 below
*Deutsche Bundesbahn: page 63
Colin Garratt/Milepost: pages 46 below, 47 below
*Finnish state railways: pages 8 right, 9 top left, 18 below
Military Archive & Research Services, Lincolnshire, England: pages 8 left, 9 right, 14, 19 left, 21, 22 below left, 23 right, 26 left and right, 27 all, 35 top, 37 right, 38 top, 39 below, 42 top and below right, 46 top both, 48 right
*Mack Trucks Inc.: page 38 below left
*National Library of Australia: page 28 left
*New Zealand Railways: pages 49 top right, 50 top
*Northern Pacific Railroad: pages 9 below, 10 left, 30, 31 below
©Railfotos, Millbrook House Limited, Oldbury, W. Midlands, England: pages 2, title pages, 4–5 (P. Harris), 7, 10 right, 11, 12 all, 13, 15 right, 16, 17, 18 top right, 19 right, 20, 22 top, 28 right, 32, 33 top left, 36, 37 left, 41 below, 42 below left, 47 top, 50 below left, 51 both, 52, 53, 54, 56 top left and below, 62
*Santa Fe Railroad: pages 40, 43 right, 48 left
*SNCF: pages 35 below right, 55 both, 57 below, 58 both
*Southern Railway: pages 50 below right, top of 56–57
*Union Pacific Railroad Museum: pages 22 below right, 23 left, 34, 38 below right

* Prints/transparencies through Military Archive & Research Services, Lincolnshire, England